REAL INTIMACY

Extended Lovemaking in the
Committed Relationship

REAL INTIMACY

Extended Lovemaking in the Committed Relationship

by Mike Devine and David Routh
Foreword by Sheelagh G. Bull, Ph.D.

──── STARSIDE ────
PUBLISHING COMPANY
OVERLAND PARK/KANSAS CITY

**FOR REORDER CALL
LADY CARLTSTON
1-800-690-5939**

C

Library of Congress Cataloging-in-Publication Data

Devine, Michael.
   Real intimacy : extended lovemaking in the committed relationship/by Michael Devine and David Routh.
   p.   cm.
   ISBN 0-9625096-0-4
   1. Sex instruction for men. I. Routh, David. II. Title.
HQ36.D48   1989   88-38277
613.9'6'024041—dc 19   CIP

Printed in the United States of America

Author's Introduction

This book will tell a man how to maintain an erection indefinitely, and how the muscular technique that allows this to happen works.

The authors of this book did not write it to be a manual on marital relations outside of the strict limits of its subject matter. While it would be very easy for us to expand it to include many generalizations about how the technique might affect a relationship, this would have little value for a large percentage of our readers. We could speculate endlessly about how Mr. X might behave differently once he understands the technique and how Mrs. X now feels about how he feels—well, you get the idea.

If we get lots of letters describing these situations, maybe we'll compile another book. In the meantime, we present *Real Intimacy* with the assumption that the necessary emotional basis for a healthy sexual relationship is already in place. The couple is not in a power-play situation—one using the deficiencies of the other to build self-esteem or to cover up insecurities.

We are not marriage counselors. We do recognize that there are many ways to build a better relationship through communication, caring, and trust. We hope that such elements will be at work in a relationship where the couple tries the technique. We highly recommend it. A lot of self-esteem in males is attached to sexual performance, and the issue is probably a volatile one in couples of any

1

age. But in any healthy relationship, both the man and woman realize that there is a wide gap between loving the other for their own worth and defining them strictly by some vague standard of sexual performance. These false standards are often based on some movie's depiction of a great lover. Love is never dependent upon your partner being a sexual athlete.

However, this book is about a physical process, and we have focused solely on that aspect of the technique. This allows us to present it in a brief, easily understood format. Our readers don't require lectures on listening to a partner's concerns. There are many published books relating to such subjects, and it would be deceptive of us to sell you a 200-page book with something as short and simple as this technique buried deep inside. That's why the volume you're holding is slim. It's our version of truth in advertising.

This book solves a physical problem. At first, the man who uses the technique will be sacrificing an orgasm to satisfy his partner's sexual needs. We say "at first" because it is possible to reach a stage where one can actually time achievement of an orgasm, although you've used the technique up to that point. We mention this towards the end of the text.

Since the beginner will initially give up an orgasm, however, we consider this a built-in guarantee that it won't be misused for selfish goals. But we don't intend to manipulate adults who can think for themselves. It's up to them to develop maturity and temperance in using this technique.

Our character, Tom, may seem egocentric. If that is the case, all improvement in a relationship is ultimately going to benefit the person making the effort. If this is selfish, it is enlightened self-interest. Some may think he is sexist or conceited because of his attitude toward pleasing a woman. He isn't. And we are keeping in the spirit of the times by emphasizing that he is happily married and faithful to his wife. The times are not such anymore to encourage sex as a recreational activity. As we say in the text, this isn't to impress a stranger with your sexual prowess.

We believe we have gone out of our way not to portray Tom as a bed-hopping egotist. If he still seems that way, search your own feelings about this subject and you may tap into some unresolved anger. This would be productive as you sort out your reactions to the new-found abilities we offer men. We are not in any way advocating promiscuity or a return to the sexual behavior patterns of the past. The sexual landscape is more dangerous than it used to be. The greatest lover in the world is capable of being so with one woman.

Foreword
by Sheelagh G. Bull, Ph.D.

Here we are at the end of the sexual revolution, in the middle of an AIDS crisis. The yuppies have given up on spending all of their time working out and partying, and are now deeply into being couch potatoes. Conservatism is on the rise, and some guy feels now is the time to tell the world about a new sexual technique. He must be out of sync. This is 1989, not 1968. We are all too tired, too busy, and too burned out on sex to care about reading any more ways to ecstasy. Right?

Wrong! This guy is right on target. Now is the right time for a book which stresses commitment, communication, process over goal, empathizing, accommodating another's needs, and intimacy.

In recent decades, people who were bored with their sex lives found a new lover. This worked great for awhile, but soon that sexual relationship paled and off the person went looking for greener pastures. It never worked very well, for all it was trumped up in the media. People looking for great sex were often really looking for intimacy, and if someone found great sex, they felt that was it. Sex is often great in the first flush of passion, and then often seems to get less satisfying and more routine as the relationship wears on. Changing partners may bring added excitement, but it rarely brings intimacy. Perhaps the sexual revolution is wearing down, because for all the bed-hopping it has become clear to people that the real problem in sexual encounters is that men and women have different rhythms. Men are ready to go and women want and (often) need a slower pace and bigger build up. Changing partners helps, or seems to help, because in first encounters there is usually a long introduction stage before the main event *or*, the seduction *is* the main event. In older relationships, this seduction is usually omitted and the woman is not ready when the man is. The whole point of this marvelous little book is to teach a man to prolong his potency, so that he can enjoy the seduction or foreplay period of lovemaking so important and essential to a woman, without losing his desire or erection. The premise of the book being that premature ejaculation is any male orgasm which occurs before the partner is ready for her orgasm. Since a man can be ready in ten minutes and a woman may want or need thirty minutes or more to climax, the author suggests that most men are or have been premature ejaculators some or all of the time. (And we've just spent twenty years in a sexual revolution?)

The technique this book teaches can be read in about five minutes. In fact, if you want to, skip right to page 39 and learn how to do it. Go ahead, be impulsive and goal-oriented. Get to the good stuff right away; miss all the really important stuff like "paying attention with all of the five senses" and "having an emotional basis for a healthy sexual relationship in place." In fact, those of you tempted to rush to page 39 and get on with it are behaving in a manner which goes against the point of this book. This book is so full of great wisdom on the real meaning and value of a good sexual relationship. Masters and Johnson called sex the pleasure bond. The author seems to delight in pointing out the advantages to a man of learning to be responsive in the way a woman is responsive; learning to emphasize, to accommodate another person's needs rather than one's own, enjoying the process rather than going for the goal, and making love—not using sex as a powerplay situation. This is not new stuff, it is very old. The Chinese talk of the tao of sex, of the importance of the sexual relationship to help the man balance his maleness with femaleness, and the woman to balance her femaleness with maleness. This little book uses everyday language to say the same thing.

This book is important because it does have a valuable technique to teach to men. But this technique is not new. The taoists in China and the yogis of India with their tantric yoga, knew thousands of years ago about the value of prolonging male potency. This technique could be learned from any of a number of esoteric, erudite, spiritually-oriented books or treatises. It could have been written in a manner appealing to the Don Juans among us, for whom this technique could become a claim to fame. But this is a gentle, loving book written by a gentle man who really respects and loves women, and believes in committed relationships. A man reading this book will gain a better understanding of the value of a woman's point of view in a relationship. He will have an opportunity to evaluate his own relationships and see if they have been characterized by a goal-oriented, performance-oriented approach to sexuality. He will discover that in learning to control his potency, he will have a "higher level of responsibility," because a good sexual relationship means he "will become emotionally and physically involved in a new way." Don Juans should read this book only at the risk of losing their egocentric approach to sexual encounters. This is a book for lovers, committed lovers, who want to keep the bond between them strong with shared ecstasy.

I am a psychologist with a private practice. Many times when I have tried to help couples with their sexual relationship I have been at a loss as to what I could give them to read. Too much of what was available and useful was too esoteric, or too ribald, or too intellectual, or too long-winded. I agreed to write the foreword to this book because I wanted to have it as a resource for my own practice. This book stresses many of the values I hold about relationships. It offers in a readable, short format not just a technique, but a way of thinking about sexual relationships which I would be comfortable sharing with my clients. Read it. Practice what it preaches, and may you enjoy with your beloved a long, ecstatic relationship.

Sheelagh G. Bull, Ph.D.
Clinical Psychologist

Real Intimacy:
The Discovery

The rain sprayed from the road as cars raced through the night in front of the downtown bar.

Steve Prentiss and Tom Newhouse sat inside catching up on the years they'd been separated since they were roommates in college. From their table by the window, they could see the rain still falling. It was early in the evening, however, and Steve and Tom had no intention of leaving the warm bar.

They had discussed the most immediate concern, Steve's upcoming wedding to Laura. Tom Newhouse would be the best man.

"You'll love being married," Tom was saying. "For one thing, you'll live longer being married."

"That's what they say about people with pets, too. But there's more responsibility with Laura than with a cat or dog," Steve said.

"Yeah, Laura's probably not as loyal as a puppy if she's known you for three years," Tom said. "She might know your faults by now."

Steve answered proudly, "Well, I don't have many. You've lasted four years with Jeannie. Isn't your honeymoon over yet?"

"No, it isn't. Certainly not the physical part. It's just as intense as when we first got married. But there's a reason for that."

"You're still taking all those vitamins," Steve

guessed.

Tom turned slightly serious. "They never were the reason for my success with the ladies."

Steve laughed. "I knew there was a reason we called you Tom Cat in college. But you'd never tell me what it was."

"I was afraid of everyone finding out. But since I'm faithful to my wife, I feel a little guilty these days. So I've decided to share my secret with a few individuals I think can be trusted."

"Is it dangerous?"

"No, just revolutionary. But I guess anything which changes people's habits runs up against resistance," Tom said.

"So what was your secret of success?"

"Prolonged male potency, to word it politely," Tom said, an embarrassed smile on his lips.

"And you'll tell me this secret?" Steve leaned forward.

"Sure," Tom answered. "Think of it as a wedding present. To prolong your honeymoon."

"Well, thank you!" Steve stopped to think for a second. "Is it a pill?"

"No, it's not a drug or a device or any chemical solution. It won't cost you a cent. It can't hurt you. And you'll never run out of it once you get it."

"Why haven't you done something with this? You could be rich."

"I might some day," Tom answered. "But it would probably upset my life, and I like my life. You see, I have fewer insecurities than other guys, and this little technique of mine is one reason why."

"And I can learn this technique?"

"Sure. I have organized this in my head in case I ever write a book. Now I don't know how embarrassed you might be by this subject, so I won't ask you dozens of questions about your sex life. I'll presume that you and

Laura are like lots of other modern couples and haven't been celibate during your courtship. This technique won't instantly guarantee perfect bliss after you're married, but it could make your sex life with Laura more compatible with her needs."

"Well, things have been okay so far," Steve said.

"That's how it is with most couples: 'okay.' I'm not saying this will make everything perfect, but it will probably make it easy for you to sexually satisfy your wife. I talked to a priest once about this, and he said that almost all the marital problems he sees end up starting with one factor—the woman isn't really sexually satisfied. And this priest really didn't know what to tell people. Men and women just seem to function differently in bed. A man achieves his goal in ten minutes while his wife might take an hour. Most men can't last that long."

"I know what that can be like," admitted Steve.

"Has it been a real problem for you? You don't have to answer that if you don't want to."

"No, it's okay," Steve said, toying with his empty beer glass. "There are ways around that problem which most couples use."

"Exactly, but somehow in the back of their minds, there's a frustration or resentment building up. Frustration for the wife and resentment for the husband. The man feels inadequate because he can't please his wife, 'the normal way.' And the woman isn't too pleased with the situation, either."

"Prolonged potency would get any guy around that problem, wouldn't it?" Steve asked.

"Yes. My technique or other forms of stimulation are the only way to satisfy a woman. Some people don't want those other forms. Jeannie and I never had that problem because I worked out the technique in college before I met her. But I wasn't the first man to make love to her, and I was quite a surprise to her, believe me!"

"And after the first time you two made love, she probably thought Clark Kent had dropped his mild manners along with his pants!"

"It didn't hurt any," Tom admitted.

"If I use this technique on my honeymoon, it'll certainly impress Laura. She'll attribute it to the romance."

"I'm afraid I need to warn you, then," Tom said. "It may require some practice. Habits are hard to break, and what a man and a woman do in bed may be one of the hardest to break. But with some practice and awareness of what you are doing I think you'll be able to last several hours if need be."

"Several hours?" Steve stared in astonishment at his old friend. "That can't really be possible!"

"It is. Few men (or women) would want to go that long, maybe. But it is possible. Once you implement the technique, however, you won't be having an orgasm as soon as usual." Tom looked around and saw the other customers in the bar weren't listening. The general noise level seemed adequate to insure their privacy.

"How is that possible?"

"Well, I first devised this technique when I ran into a girl in college who simply couldn't achieve what I took for granted during our lovemaking. She just never experienced an orgasm. Nothing worked. So I got to thinking about what I could do to make myself last longer. I meditated on this a while and studied male potency some." Tom stopped and looked around for the waitress. Not seeing her, he continued. "So if you want to get involved in this, there are some things we need to go over. Between studying, sleep-thinking, and testing each new idea I came up with every two days, it's a miracle I even maintained a B average in college. But I had a lot of fun testing those ideas.

"This girlfriend in college was a farm girl and very

honest with me. I was her first, uh, partner, and she was frank about things. It's thanks to her honesty that I made this discovery. I think lots of the girls I knew may have been very good actresses. Years later, they could still be acting even after having children.

"And even Laura could be one of those actresses, Steve. Many a husband never knows his wife's real thoughts because it's a difficult subject to talk about, even among people who are supposedly 'liberated.'"

"Come on, get to the point," Steve said.

The Categories

"As I was saying, if you want to get involved in this, there are some things we need to go over. I've made up categories I put guys into, in case I ever reveal this publicly and need to apply it to everyone. The first category is the red category. Men go in the red category if they have problems getting an erection. I can't help a fellow in that situation. If you were in that category, the only thing I could tell you would be to seek professional help.

"The next category is the yellow category. These are guys who can keep it up for just around ten or twenty minutes before they have an orgasm during intercourse. The yellow category is probably the most typical one. Most men just fall into this category. There's nothing wrong with that. It's the norm.

"The yellow category is what I'm focusing on. The guy in the yellow category who has a woman with high sexual needs probably has a problem, and my technique is what he may need. He may need an extra day a week off if he learns my technique!" Tom laughed.

"The next category," he continued, "is the green one. This is for guys who can keep an erection between thirty and forty-five minutes, and beyond, during intercourse. These are men who may need or want to know my technique eventually. These guys are already using the technique subconsciously and aren't even aware of it. A guy I talked to once didn't know how he did it. He couldn't control how long he kept his erection, but sometimes it was a real long time. He didn't have free will over it. The green category men may vary in their ability to maintain an erection. Sometimes they may be able to keep it up all night or maybe only half an hour. Of course, half an hour seems like forever in the red or yellow category. Still, the man in the green category will be able to have stability in his control with my technique. This gives you a choice. You can either implement the technique and therefore last a long time or ignore it and function as you would regularly. This technique gives a man control over a function which is normally considered involuntary or the next worst thing to involuntary— occasionally voluntary.

"Over and above these categories that you have to fit yourself into, there's the question of how many orgasms a man can have in one night or afternoon or morning." Tom shrugged. "Some men are capable of only one."

Steve asked, "I thought you said something earlier about not having an orgasm with your technique."

Tom answered, "That's right. Would you be in the once-a-night category or the more-than-once-a-night group?"

Steve laughed but said only, "Why don't you tell me about both groups?"

"Okay. I won't press you into embarrassing revelations. If you're in the once-a-night group, then you're going to have to make a decision. Do you want to give up your orgasm for that evening in the interest of pleasing your wife if your lack of endurance has been a problem between both of you? What my technique will do is give you the time to not worry about keeping your erection once you get it. For many, once you've got an erection you have to hurry up and finish the business at hand before it disappears. Everything's the big rush, and that's why millions of women are left unsatisfied. If you're a once-a-nighter, I've got something else to get into later. If you're twice a night or better, you're in the lucky group. A guy in that group could go ahead and have his orgasm and then implement the technique for Round Two afterwards. He could then go ahead and satisfy his partner. This is how the technique takes the pressure off your performance. I'll get into that later, too."

Two Approaches

"Steve, there's two ways you need to start this. You should ask Laura if your keeping an erection much longer would help satisfy her, because it could be that she's like a lot of women. She might not be telling you the whole story about the extent of her sexual needs. She might tell you that having you keep it up a lot longer would be just what the doctor ordered, and this would prompt you to surprise her with a little sneak attack once you're armed with this knowledge. If you implement this technique without telling her and last several hours, you will probably leave her terribly sore from the experience and she'll feel that perhaps she can't satisfy *your* needs. Don't do this.

"During an extended lovemaking session you might want her to switch positions with you or stop or whatever is necessary, but remember that you won't be having an orgasm. I don't recommend a sneak attack where a man tries this without consulting his partner, because the woman will feel she can't satisfy him. In your case, Steve, this would be especially bad if you gave Laura that impression right when you're starting married life together.

"Oh, after using the technique on your honeymoon, after you've stopped you won't be able to dash out of the hotel room and run down to the beach. You'll still have an erection for about fifteen minutes. If I didn't tell you this now you could have a really bad scare that first time. It might seem like you'll never get rid of it. But believe me, it will go down after a while. Just relax and wait. It could be longer than fifteen minutes, too."

Tom sat back and thought for a second. "I said there were two ways to start this. The other thing you have to remember is, well, remember when you had that old orange Volkswagen back in college that could only top out at sixty-five miles per hour? And then your Dad bought you that XKE that could easily hit a hundred and forty miles per hour? Your Dad bought you that car because you got straight A's. But he trusted you with that power and he believed you had the maturity to handle it wisely. You didn't try driving a hundred and forty around the campus. So here I am trusting you to handle the power of this technique wisely. You did run that XKE at the race track now and then. You might want to use this technique just as sparingly. Like every two weeks. This can be rather addictive for you—or for her. There's time for quickies and then there's time for the Indy 500, to mix a metaphor. Don't go on a power trip with this. Communicate with Laura and don't abuse this knowledge. That's something I would tell anyone I shared this with."

Tom continued, "I don't want to invade your privacy too much, but hasn't Laura ever not had an orgasm and still told you afterwards that she loved it and got a really nice high? Maybe it wasn't an orgasm, but it was just as good as one."

"Yeah, she's done that," Steve admitted.

"I thought so. Most women I've talked to have related that little experience. Steve, Laura wasn't lying to you. Many men think women are lying when they say that, but women really can have a high that way. And what I call that high is a climax. Men usually associate climax with an orgasm because the two usually occur simultaneously. That's why men don't believe what a woman says. Steve, this will probably be the first time, using the technique, that you'll experience a climax without having an orgasm. Climaxes are unique in a way since they start low and build up and happen one after the other. If you're that once-a-night fellow, you won't be forfeiting all the excitement to your wife if you implement the technique and make love. The best way to describe these highs or climaxes is like rolling waves getting bigger and bigger."

Steve said, "It sounds like you've talked to a lot of people."

"I have," Tom said. "I've talked to lots of couples about this. I didn't mean to give you the impression that you're the very first guy I've talked to. I've had to do research on this, you know."

"What fun research."

"Some of it's hard work. Anyway, after you've learned this technique you will be able to have even more openness with Laura about your sex life. And that will affect other parts of your relationship. It will benefit your marriage as a whole. This will be your own sexual revolution."

"I think it sounds a lot better than the sexual revolution we used to read so much about," Steve observed.

"It is. The sexual revolution everyone was proclaiming to the heavens was really just the pill and freedom from pregnancy. When that came about, lots of people started sleeping together, but all that activity was hectic and associated with singles bars and one-night stands. I don't think communication was very important to that process of a change in society. If I give my technique to the public, I would hope that men wouldn't use it without discussing it with their partners. I would hate to think that men would misuse this gift to attempt to impress women with their endurance. If they did, they wouldn't deserve the credit," Tom said.

"Well, that's what I was using my XKE for. I think every guy wants to impress women, one way or another. But what good was my XKE when you had a secret like this to help your popularity with females?" Steve asked.

"My technique wasn't the only thing that helped me with the ladies. I tried to empathize with them and see through their eyes. I realized their needs might not be exactly the same as my own. I thought this was a perfectly logical thing to do, but I guess I was some sort of strange exception to the rule."

Steve nodded. "You bought my Volkswagen from me after I got the XKE, but you still did twice as good as me. Now I see why girls were always hooked on you. You weren't just outperforming the other guys. You were communicating with your girlfriends."

Tom admitted, "I was a little immature back then. I was proud of what I could do. But I was doing my research, so I always talked about these things. Girls liked that." Tom looked around and saw the waitress approaching.

Tom and Steve ordered another beer, and Steve used the occasion to visit the restroom.

Upon his return, Steve sat down behind a cold glass of beer. "Do you think the world is ready for your discovery?"

"I think so, or else I wouldn't have come up with it. Everything has its place and time. That girlfriend off the farm in college told me that if my technique was published 'it would change humanity as we know it today.' It wouldn't change everything, obviously, but sex is terribly important to a lot of people, and I guess it would be a strange improvement if we could take the element of chance out of it as far as male performance is concerned."

The Search

"You know, you're driving me up a wall waiting for the actual details of the technique. So what is the technique? It's not a drug or an aphrodisiac or a device." Steve stopped for a second. "It has to be something muscular."

Tom smiled. "You're getting hot. Yes. But I have to warn you, if you don't do this right you won't be able to keep an erection. You'll do worse, in fact. You'll lose it."

Steve frowned. "How could that be?"

Tom said, "Steve, you're not really ready yet. I used to be in the yellow category myself. I didn't last so long. I mentioned that girlfriend in college who got me started on my studies in sexology. It certainly wasn't my intention when I started. I was after what every college guy is after. This girlfriend, not Jeannie, remember, was sort of reluctant at first when we were going together. You know how that is. I had to work on convincing her to, uh, consummate our relationship. By the time I would get her undressed and me undressed, we had already spent over half an hour in this sort of foreplay with clothes on, so it didn't take a whole lot of activity to get me more than excited enough. Almost *too* excited, if you know what I mean.

"As I discovered all too soon, this was the girlfriend who had trouble enjoying anything about our lovemaking. I could tell that she wasn't having an orgasm for all my efforts. I knew what a woman is like during that experience, but this young lady didn't show any signs. So I naturally started feeling real guilty about seducing her. If she enjoyed it, I could pat myself on the back. But instead, she was right off the farm and here I was...And since I really did love her, since she wasn't just a *date*, I wanted her to enjoy everything I felt during our lovemaking. That's when I started to sleep-think on this problem."

Steve took a sip of his beer and asked, "Sleep-think? What's that?"

"I'll get to that, too. So this girlfriend gave me a real challenge. She was what you would call old-fashioned. Like I said, she'd been raised on a farm in Nebraska. And when she finally decided to give in to my little demands, she wanted to make love the way they do in the movies. So that precluded any oral or manual stimulation on my part, which is how you normally take care of a problem like that. She knew she wasn't enjoying our lovemaking, so she asked me to figure out what she needed. But look at the conditions she gave me. Nothing oral, nothing manual, and nothing mechanical. That left out anything but normal foreplay to get her excited. This left the entire responsibility on you-know-what part of my anatomy. That's just the way it worked out.

"Of course," Tom continued, "she was so beautiful that once she was undressed, I was close to the edge already. Obviously, something had to be done. And me in the yellow category! The only information I could work with, since I didn't do that much reading on the subject, was based on prior knowledge. I had no idea how to solve this problem. I could have just walked away from it, but I really did care about Martha. That was the girl from Nebraska. But another girl was the clue to Martha's solution.

"This goes back to the first girl I ever went to bed with. That first girl dictated the terms of our little rendezvous that night. We had foreplay, but this is what she actually did. She kissed me, with me naked, for about forty-five minutes. When we finally got around to the inevitable, I'd had three consecutive orgasms and never lost my erection. Even driving her home I never lost my erection. Later, I just figured this was a once-in-a-lifetime thing that could never be duplicated."

"But you did duplicate it, huh?" Steve asked.

"Don't rush things. Good things come to those who wait. But we're going back to Martha, yeah. I worked consciously on prolonging intercourse with her because of this problem. When I slowed down or stopped, though, Martha would lose all previous excitement built up. It was like taking an elevator back to the ground floor each time. And she told me this. That was her typical honesty. She was a good research partner. But this left me back at square one, although the research was quite enjoyable. Martha did want results eventually."

"You didn't stall just for the hell of it?" Steve asked.

"Oh, no. In case you've never had that happen to you, making love to a woman without bringing her any pleasure seemed totally unfair. That was what spurred me on to work out something to our mutual agreement. So I started mentally reviewing my experiences. The only thing that stuck in my mind was that time with the girl who kissed me all over. Had I done something physical to cause that reaction in my genitals? If I'd done it once—and it was a physical thing you could see—then it had to be possible to duplicate it. It became like a scientific experiment to reproduce the conditions that created that reaction.

"So every time I went to sleep, I'd go over every second of the experience with that first girl. For months I did a mental rerun. This was the only piece of real evidence I ever had. So each time I'd come up with some new answer, Martha and I would try it out. She knew what I was doing. This day-by-day discussion and experimentation led to a lot of communication and openness. So you want to know how the sleep-thinking worked?" Tom asked.

"I'd rather hear the technique right now. But you've got me intrigued with that, too, I'm sorry to say," Steve added. He made a sour face to indicate he understood the delay it might cause before his ultimate enlightment.

"Well, before I'd go to sleep—alone, that is—I'd think about an answer before I fell asleep. I might wake up two or three times during the night or just wake up normally in the morning. Each time I woke up I'd have some kind of answer. I was programming my brain to solve a problem. I was locking it in on 'compute' so I wouldn't have to mess with it during my waking state.

"In the middle of the night if I woke up, if I didn't write it down, I'd have another idea when I woke up. So I'd have to get up in the middle of the night and write down my idea right then. Of course, some of those notes were pretty hard to read the next morning! I probably lost a few good ideas that way, but I found the one that worked. Steve, let me tell you why that's so important.

"I woke up one morning with the idea and didn't write it down. And it probably took me six or seven weeks again to find it. Eventually, the same idea came back, but we're talking about a year and a half after Martha first agreed to let me try to find an answer to her dilemma. I'll confess I probably spent more time naked with Martha than I did in school. Of course, later on Martha started talking to her friends. Some of them shared her problem. They discussed it without being as embarrassed about the whole thing the way guys are.

"You know, women are a lot more honest about these things than men are. Men have their macho image to protect. Women don't, thank God! Otherwise, I'd never have figured out what to do to help Martha.

"One idea I tried, the one I'd lost for six or seven weeks, I wrote down one night in my sleep when it came back. I read the notes later which had been written in the dark, and I almost couldn't decipher the awful scribbles on the pad. I did figure them out and went over to Martha's room at the dorm and we tried it. And it worked so well it scared me. Steve, you'll never believe this. After about an hour Martha was still unsatisfied. Of course, she was getting real sore, so we had to resort to a lubricant. An hour and a half later she finally had and orgasm. This was the total time we'd been making love. Two and a half hours! And it was the most pleasure I've ever witnessed a person having. It was beautiful. It was like seeing a baby born. Fifteen minutes after intercourse, I still had an erection which I doubted would ever go down."

The Technique

Steve looked down at his beer glass. "That would sure be a nice memory to come back to in later years. So what exactly is the great secret of this technique?"

"Okay, here it is," Tom said. "The technique itself is rather simple. For me to explain the technique, let me go back to the logic behind what I found in sleep-thinking. This may sound like something way out in left field. Anything I try, if I don't get a good result in a problem-solving situation, I automatically think of the exact opposite. The most opposite thing I could think of from having intercourse was urinating. You might guess that it's very difficult to urinate with a full erection. I'm basing this on the premise that the urinary tract is blocked off by an erection.

"This set of circumstances," Tom continued, "was the premise for my discovery. The logic behind the technique relies on that condition. The blockage of the urinary tract during an erection can serve a purpose. So let me explain this a bit."

Tom seemed in the middle of a memorized speech. He took a sip of beer. "What I discovered was a link between the muscles you associate mentally with relaxation for urination. By using those muscles correctly—not to urinate or attempt to urinate but to isolate and flex those muscles properly, you can achieve amazing results.

"That's what I did when I finally succeeded. To my

delight and astonishment my erection did not go down. Since I've been using the technique—well, you're not going to believe this. Steve, I've kept up an erection off and on for as long as six hours."

"You're right. I don't believe that. You should be in the Guinness Book of World Records."

"I don't think they have an entry for that record," Tom observed. "Or one for women who can make love that long."

"I bet Casanova himself couldn't last that long."

"I may end up calling this the Casanova technique, now that you mention him."

"But what good is a six-hour erection?" Steve asked.

"Not a whole lot. You have to bear in mind that most women will wear out in about two and a half hours if not a lot earlier."

"Well, now I know what you were talking about when you made that analogy to my old Volkswagen versus the XKE."

"Okay, so after we're through here tonight, don't take this new 'XKE' and drive it into the ground. Just remember not to lose your head. This knowledge, like any other kind, brings responsibility. If you go for six hours, you'll want to sleep for twenty-four. You'll feel like you've been waterskiing that long. I don't recommend that you go that long, and I doubt that Laura would ever want to go that long. And remember that this isn't going to be for your satisfaction—it's for hers. And now that you're armed with this knowledge, trying for a new marathon record could do more harm than good in your marriage. After all, you've got to get Laura's opinion of all this once I'm done explaining everything to you."

"You're right," Steve said. "I don't think she'd appreciate six hours of even *that*."

Tom grinned. "Somebody once told me that the quality of a carpenter's hammer will not directly reflect in the quality of his work. The secret lies in how he swings the hammer. You have to know something about timing and the mood when a longer session might be appropriate. *This isn't for every night.* You need to know your own endurance and Laura's time requirements for an orgasm. And you need to be paying attention with all five senses.

"What this does is take the stress of performance off of you. When you get an erection you won't be worried about losing it before you and she are satisfied. And that in itself ought to open up a whole new field of enjoyment."

Steve added, "And this would take the pressure off of Laura to have an orgasm during *my* time limit before I have one. She could relax and enjoy it without feeling she's working under the gun. The whole thing would stop being an obligation."

"That's right. Steve, you have to apply this correctly. None of this will work otherwise. You'll think you've learned something interesting without having it work for you in particular. This information won't work alone and you could get very bad results. This should be in a simple step-by-step approach. But prior to that, to learn the step-by-step technique, you'll have to bear in mind that when you have sex with Laura, for the past year or whatever in addition to other past experiences of yours, you've formulated a pattern or habit. Before, you've had sex with only thinking, rather emotionally, about your two bodies together. Now what you need is some mental self-control. I'm only talking about using the technique when necessary, which is only a small fraction of the total time when you would be engaged in intercourse. Don't get confused. I'm not saying it's a mental thing. It's a physical control. You need a physical control at the beginning of sex in order to implement the technique. And it's not something that you'll have to continue doing during the entire time you're having intercourse. It's

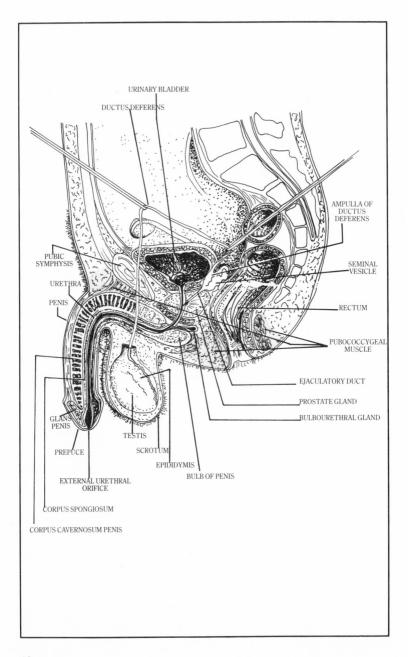

URINARY BLADDER

DUCTUS DEFERENS

AMPULLA OF
DUCTUS
DEFERENS

PUBIC
SYMPHYSIS

SEMINAL
VESICLE

URETHRA

PENIS

RECTUM

PUBOCOCCYGEAL
MUSCLE

EJACULATORY DUCT

PROSTATE GLAND

BULBOURETHRAL GLAND

GLANS
PENIS

TESTIS

PREPUCE

SCROTUM

EPIDIDYMIS

BULB OF PENIS

EXTERNAL URETHRAL
ORIFICE

CORPUS SPONGIOSUM

CORPUS CAVERNOSUM PENIS

something at the beginning.

"As I was saying about habits, your habit has always been to be certain to have an orgasm before your erection goes down. Now I'm talking about caring enough about Laura to focus on *her* from now on, and her orgasms. The habit I'm talking about is a habit you've formulated to bring about an orgasm in you in ten minutes. To implement the technique is contrary to your old habit. And based on all the emotion you have when you're engaged in sex with Laura, it takes practice to have self control. So it may not work the first time you try it.

"That may be one factor that's involved. And there is only really one other. The other one is isolating that muscle or group of muscles that you need to be pushing with."

"Does it have a name?" Steve asked.

"Actually, I guess we're talking about the pubococcygeal muscle. I've got a book at home that recommends locating this muscle with a woman flexing against a finger in her vagina or a man flexing against a finger in his rectum. Most men aren't interested in that kind of activity, including me. It reminds me of a proctological examination I once had. That book recommended a meditative exercise before concentrating on that muscle and learning to exercise it. The meditation was to help clear the mind before locating the muscle, and that helped eliminate the old habits which confuse you.

"The best way, in fact, for a guy to locate the muscle, in my opinion, is just while you're sitting there, try to pull up on your anus. When you flex that whole muscle, the lower part of your stomach will also flex in as well. This comprises the whole muscle.

"As for location, the front side of the muscle exists as well as the backside of it behind you. Every muscle has a corresponding opposite. There's a push and pull in front of this muscle for urinating and a push and pull in back for defecating. If you lift up on that entire muscle, your buttocks will close up together and your anus rises up. While urinating, your urine flow would then stop.

"I don't know much about this muscle in technical terms, but spending some time locating these (especially the front one) will be imperative. The push and pull are the most important thing in the front set. Pushing the front muscle will make you feel your testicles lower or make it feel like you're pushing them down. And the anus will contract up.

"The opposite occurs," Tom continued, "when you attempt to stop urinating when you cut off the flow with your muscles. That's a pulling sensation.

"The opposite is a pushing sensation. It feels almost identical. It feels like you're pulling, almost the same sensation as when you push the remaining urine out of your penis at the end of urinating. Your anus reacts the same way each time, going up, when you either push that muscle or pull it.

"Remember back in grade school or later when you had to urinate but you waited until class was over because you were embarrassed? And then you went to the restroom and couldn't urinate? Or *at first* you couldn't urinate which is sometimes the case. That is caused by the same muscle. When you urinate, you push that muscle the same as you would with my technique. But all the time you held in the urine, that muscle was in use, and I think you were really locking in a *very* slight erection and preventing urination later. That's the same as the technique without the full erection.

"Going back to that sensation of pushing out with that muscle, you should focus on that function since it's the key to my technique. With an erection, I've been able to make my penis jerk upwards a little bit. I can move it to a certain degree but not very much."

"So what does that mean?" Steve asked.

"That's the exact muscle I use for the technique. When I'm pulling in that front muscle, that makes my erection flex. That's the opposite of the motion you need to implement the technique. You need to push out to start the technique. You can practice flexing the muscles isometrically anywhere, since they are flexed internally and there is no need for weights or exercises. That will help you locate them, and also strengthen them for later use.

"I tell people there are four steps to my technique. The first step is that you absolutely must have a full erection before you start the procedure. How you want to assure this is your own business, or course, but be absolutely certain you *do* have a full erection because you will be locking it in at a *slightly* smaller size once you've succeeded.

"The second step then is for you to receive direct stimulation in some form for two minutes or more depending on how long you usually can last. Here's a guide for you. If after foreplay and ten minutes of intense stimulation like intercourse you usually have an orgasm, then I'd recommend you wait two minutes after the start of intercourse before implementing the technique. A general scale would be about one-fifth of the way through your normal endurance. So if you normally go for half an hour, then you need to start the technique after six minutes.

"If you don't wait this important interval, and it may vary slightly for individuals, then you will have some definite problems. If you don't have a complete erection prior to implementation of the technique, you may go limp. You've cut off the blood supply before it was adequate. Remember this point and don't panic if you make a mistake when you are learning.

"Also, you have to think about what you're doing. You'll have to stop and think, and this will take you out of the erotic atmosphere you've created. You may get serious about this. But this technique should only take a few seconds, and Laura won't even know it since this will run so quickly through your mind once you've practiced. Don't try to stop everything and make a big production. Do it so she doesn't even know it's happening.

"Another thing is, don't create stress for yourself. You can't learn how to do something perfectly the very first time you try. So don't expect that to happen with my technique. It probably won't. You've got plenty of time to perfect your control."

"So don't rush things and have fun, right?" Steve asked.

"Exactly. You've got plenty of time, and all the time you spend perfecting your control should be relaxed and pleasurable. Don't turn this into an absolute 'must' that adds stress to your sex life. This part of your life is something that should not be hurried and goal-oriented. It may take some practice to make the whole process run smoothly. The technique will not force you to stop everything dead, so it won't be a stumbling block. Instead, it will take the pressure off of you during lovemaking.

"Next, flex the pelvic area muscle that you move when you urinate. This is the pushing out effort with that front part of the muscle that I was talking about earlier. You should be pushing hard enough so you can hold it only for two to four seconds before it automatically relaxes. If you can push it longer, then you are *not* pushing hard enough. It will automatically relax if you do. Then you need to repeat this process right away consecutively two or three times. This will insure that you have begun the proper use of the technique. Without this repetition you may not be on the road to success.

"The fourth step is a type of insurance. It is necessary to maintain your erection for the lengths of time I've promised you. Repeat the flexing process two or three times after the first five minutes. After that, you should flex that muscle two or three times every fifteen to twenty minutes during sustained intercourse or stimulation.

It may even take seven to ten repetitions each interval, which is what I use. It may differ from you, and you made need to tailor it to suit your needs. If you haven't flexed enough times or often enough, then you might go ahead and have an orgasm like you normally do. Of course, this isn't a disaster. This is what you do anyway, so enjoy it.

"If you've started the technique correctly and you're doing this for your wife, after fifteen minutes you won't be able to have an orgasm. And you shouldn't try. This would only hurt you and Laura by exhausting yourself needlessly.

"If you wish to have an orgasm after prolonging your endurance, then you will have to allow your erection to subside. It may take five minutes or up to twenty minutes for it to go away. Then you need to wait at the very least an hour, and it wouldn't be a bad idea just to wait until the next morning or evening or whatever. The point is—give yourself a break. Don't exhaust yourself and think that this technique is going to give you energy you don't have.

"As I said earlier, this is for a special occasion now and then. Don't attempt to use this every other night. That would simply be counterproductive. That's not why I came up with it.

"This technique is good for couples who wish to time their lovemaking, to synchronize it. It can be used in any position you desire. For a woman who needs more attention and stimulation, this may make it possible finally for the husband to last that long. That doesn't mean he'll always need to use the technique, but it can eliminate the kinds of frustration that hurt a marriage.

He'll have true sexual confidence finally, and he won't feel that he has somehow failed even though he's been completely normal or average in his performance. The couple will no longer be laboring under the deadline of the timing of his orgasm. This takes the stress off her as well, since she won't feel hurried. Both will be in a much more relaxed state. They can enjoy and explore themselves to a greater degree."

NOTE: When the penis is fully erect, it is almost impossible for the male to urinate.

T   F

TRUE. The penis has two *separate* functions: urination and reproduction. During ejaculation, a small valve automatically closes the opening between the urethra canal and bladder so effectively that it is impossible in the healthy male for urine to escape through the penis during *ejaculation*. This also makes it difficult to urinate while a man has a full erection.

Erotic Focus, A New Way to Enhance Your Sexual Pleasure, Barbara DeBetz, M.D. and Samm Sinclair Baker, NAL Books, 1985, pp. 8, 12-13.

Communication

"Much of my technique is really something that men have acquired and known subconsciously all their lives. And about sixty percent of all men have the ability but don't have direct control over it all the time. If they've had a good day, it won't be a problem. They know it subconsciously. Since it's held in their subconscious mind, they can't control when or how long they need stimulation to make it work. As soon as they learn it consciously with these steps they'll be able to use it naturally and easily. But they've always had a limitation of an orgasm after even thirty to forty-five minutes. A small portion of that group may have a longer endurance ability."

"I wonder if Laura is ready for all this," Steve muttered. "You know she might get terribly sore."

"That's right," Tom told his friend. "The most important thing that goes along with my technique is communication. There is a higher level of responsibility once you gain this kind of endurance. Armed with this knowledge, you'll be very caught up in sex for long periods of time and become emotionally and physically involved in a new way. I've made love to women for long periods of time. After an hour and a half, if my partner is panting and groaning and hyperventilating, I'll stop. I'll be in control, after all, with my technique while my partner may be enjoying herself as she normally would only for a protracted length of time. I do this with Jeannie.

"What you and Laura should do," Tom suggested, "is establish a set of signals between the two of you to be used during sex. One signal would be verbal—and the best word is STOP. The other signal would be nonverbal, and that might be something like having her hit you twice with her fist on your back or anywhere else. She needs a way to tell you to stop even if she can't put it into words. If Laura is panting and gasping for air, stop and ask her if it's okay. Most times she'll tell you not to stop.

"But remember you're driving an XKE that's been revved up. The XKE is you. Use about one-fourth of the abilities you've gained through the technique."

"Is the technique going to work as a contraceptive then? Laura was going to stop using the pill, and I was thinking about the honeymoon...."

"Oh, God, no! This isn't a contraceptive measure. I've had women ask me since I wasn't going to have an orgasm if they could then go off the pill. I've told them I have no idea about it, but anyone who asks me that really isn't showing good judgment. It's common knowledge, unless you count teenagers who have no idea what they're doing, that a woman can easily get pregnant from intercourse even if the man doesn't ejaculate. Anyone with this knowledge needs to use *both* good judgment and lots of communication with their partner.

"After all, the word intercourse means communication. And I certainly hope we'll re-establish that original meaning of the word, rather than perpetuating the stupid singles-bar games of trying to score with a complete stranger with no intention of opening up two people to each other's thoughts or emotions."

"You've changed a lot since we were roommates, that's for sure," Steve remarked.

"Well, that happened because of a few little episodes that occurred from hanging out in bars. Once word got around a few times among a certain circle of ladies, I found myself in a really strange situation. And I wasn't ready for it. Suddenly, the roles were reversed. Women were after me just for my body, and I just couldn't handle it. It was too weird. It was really hard for me to shake them. And that was my fault, too. I impressed them with this charged-up 'XKE' and I hadn't explained a thing to them. They totally misunderstood, and it was my fault. One girl in particular was positive I was deeply in love with her because of this constant erection I had when we were together in bed. I had to tell her about the technique. But I don't think it was easy for her to understand the difference between sexual arousal and love.

"These little adventures changed me real fast! I had to learn how to communicate and respect women just so I could live with myself. I wasn't trying to break a bunch of hearts although I certainly had the opportunity.

"Once I knew a lady who misinterpreted my use of the technique. She thought I wasn't being sexually satisfied even if she was. I guess she blamed herself in some way for that. It was really my fault for not explaining everything to her ahead of time. If I were single still and in similar situations, I would always tell my partner first.

"And another lady took it as a real challenge. Even though I told her I was delaying my orgasm, I think she disliked the lack of control on her part. Soon she stopped having anything to do with me because of this 'failure.'

"Anyway, that was another miserable little chapter in my education. My mistake was using the technique at all with her, because she just couldn't stand a challenge. You see, she'd heard about me through the grapevine and wanted to disprove the rumors. She didn't, of course.

"That's why I started thinking that the technique was better if used very sparingly. I got a different climactic enjoyment, of course, when I did use it.

"The real issue is that the technique *seems*, repeat, *seems* to reverse the traditional roles between men and women. People perceive it that way. Traditionally, women have had the upper hand through the ages because they could easily outlast a man during sexual intercourse, although they were rarely satisfied by it. Now it would seem that I've gained a great deal of control over them for the first time, but that's not my intention at all. It's true, however, that I've succeeded in removing that awful time limit men have worked under—the time before your orgasm arrived.

"The benefits from this technique amount to several things. First of all, the benefit to women is that if they're slow to have an orgasm and they want intercourse only, then this will finally allow them to experience it with their partners and still achieve an orgasm eventually beyond the old time limit which hindered the man. Plus you can use the technique when there's a long weekend or vacation for the couple. When the pressures of work or family do let up, here's the opportunity to use that time in a novel way to re-establish intimacy that had lapsed because of that male time limit."

"It would certainly make foreplay less of a hassle," Steve said.

"You've thought foreplay was a hassle?"

"Sure. That time limit you're talking about. Why get me all excited with an erection and then tease me for half an hour, when all I want to do is hurry up and get to the serious work before the damn thing goes down?!"

"I've heard of that same problem before from women frustrated because they want more foreplay but their husbands don't last long."

"No wonder." Steve toyed with his beer glass.

"Well, sure. Every guy has some anxiety about performance. And extended foreplay, if it's intense enough to prolong an erection for very long, can push a man's endurance limit too far. But with my technique, men will now be able, *finally*, to concentrate on the same things women have had to content themselves with for ages. Put yourself in a woman's shoes. You have sex with a guy who comes and then falls over asleep right afterwards. So what do you concentrate on? The intimacy, anticipation, caressing, stroking, kissing, and feeling the man accomplish his goal even though you won't share it. Well, that's everything there is to sex and love without the orgasm. And it's ninety percent of it, isn't it? So now men and women can share that. From now on, a man can and should experience with a woman all those other important aspects of sexuality women have concentrated on for so long. Although guys probably thought they had the better end of the deal, they may discover what they've been missing. Foreplay for a really long time now can help couples regain lost intimacy, and it will be therapeutic for men in stressful jobs to take time out to do nothing but enjoyable physical contact with a female, without that orgasm as a goal to rush to. For once, a man can just enjoy and give, rather than having an orgasm as one more item on his 'Things to Do Today' list.

"When a man has that old stress hanging over him all the time, it also puts stress on the woman although he might not notice it. An insensitive man might ask, well, if she's not going to come anyway, so what would be her time limit? Well, the woman only has ten minutes to enjoy that intimacy. Ten minutes isn't very long to share touching, kissing, and all those other goodies. Women get doubly cheated that way, see? I hope I can change all that," Tom explained.

"You'll have to write a book."

"I'm not a writer. But I probably will," Tom admitted. "I'm sure I will. When I write it, I'm going to have to put all this advice in. And not just for someone about to get married like you, Steve. If a guy was single

55

and sexually active, I'd warn him not to use this technique without plenty of communication. For one thing, he'd probably end up with women chasing him around like I had. Some of those encounters would end up in marriage proposals because women aren't really used to being sexually satisfied adequately by a man. I mean marriage proposals from women, you understand," Tom added, reading a momentary puzzlement on Steve's face.

"What would you suggest?"

"That they fall in love first and then develop a sexual relationship afterwards when sex doesn't seem so overwhelming. How many great partnerships have been short-circuited before their time because something went wrong in bed before communication had really started? With my technique, it's especially important to establish communication."

"It's not easy even when you've got a woman who's supposedly liberated," Steve confessed.

"Or a man," Tom said. "That reminds me of my uncle. He said that men should be forced to wear a chastity belt for the first five years of their marriage."

"Lord, why?" Steve asked in shock.

"You can figure that out," Tom said. He laughed. "We won't make *you* try it, though."

"Boy, that's a big relief."

"Well, a man should wear a chastity belt so he'll learn how to experience pleasure with his wife, and give her pleasure, without using his sex organ. Later on, he might need all those skills if he loses his potency. That does happen to a lot of men, and it shouldn't be the end of their sex lives, odd as that sounds. Especially not for their wives. A guy has lots of equipment besides the obvious, and most women prefer the intimacy over the actual thrill of sex if they have to make a choice. Or if they've been non-orgasmic.

"A woman can decrease that time lag for herself

through work with her husband. That might vary from year to year, but eventually a couple might synchronize themselves so that the technique itself might not even be necessary."

"How could that be?" Steve asked.

"Well, having brought this to the conscious mind from the subconscious previously, you could now take this control and actually return it to the subconscious again. After a year or two, you could use the technique subconsciously. It would revert to that level—the control of those muscles would become automatic again. If it still takes Laura forty-five minutes to achieve an orgasm, then you'll be able to last that long for her without paying much attention to it."

"Would that mean I'd be having an orgasm simultaneously with Laura? That's the way it happens in the movies."

"It'll happen in real life, too. But this is the advanced stuff we're getting into. And you haven't really worked up to that yet. That's a category beyond the ones I mentioned when we first sat down here tonight."

"Where exactly are you, then?" Steve asked, beginning to see the light.

"I'm beyond that stage. To put it another way, you have yet to learn how to walk. What I do is like running. I'm just further along."

"I don't believe there's much more to learn."

"You don't? Well, let me give you a clue. I can time myself looking at a clock as to when during sex I want to have my orgasm. If I had to, I could time myself to a certain point within fifteen minutes. You can't concern yourself with this, however, or you'll mess up your own progress. So forget it. You, like everyone else, will want to hurry through everything to get to an advanced point, but remember that I said in a *year or two* you might be able to control subconsciously when you achieve an orgasm. That won't happen in a month, and you'll be timed to certain habits with Laura. And these habits will influence your progress. Especially since you're probably in the yellow category. Don't forget this. It may take a year or two for you to reach the advanced point.

"There is an advanced and super-advanced category, but you need to concentrate on satisfying your wife instead of worrying about what happens next. Don't anticipate. After all, you can have lots of fun in your regular studies.

"Speaking of the subconscious, even men in the green category who can last half an hour or all night don't have direct control all of the time. With this information, they may be able to move into an advanced degree of timing in a month or two, and I mean achieving an orgasm when they wish to. They'd had this innate ability, but I would be giving them conscious control over it rather than the subconscious control they've had all along."

"Sounds like you've got more than one book to write," Steve commented.

"I do. But powerful medicine must be ladled out in little doses." Tom smiled. "Mustn't rush things. Oh, and speaking of medicine, I would have to put in the book that its readers should check with their family physician to be sure for their own peace of mind that the technique is safe. Men who'd had surgery near the important muscles or prostate trouble or hernias probably shouldn't try the technique unless approved by their specialist."

"What will you call the book? *Real Intimacy?* It's really about that."

"Sure. That's a good title."

"Are you going to put your real name on it?" Steve asked.

"Sure. What's wrong with Newhouse? After all, it roughly translates as *casa nova.*

"You probably were," Steve said. "You got your reward when the women started chasing *you*. When am I going to get to move into graduate school?"

"I'll meet you right here at this bar in a month."

"It's a deal. But you'll have to let me pay for the drinks," Steve warned his best man. "After sitting here tonight, I think I owe it to you."

"That's fair. By that time, you'll have finished your apprenticeship."

"No pun on my name, naturally," Steve Prentiss remarked as he rose from his chair.

"Of course not. By the way, not a word of this at the bachelor party. I don't want to have to go through this whole routine again. That won't make for much of a party if I do." Tom laid bills on the table to pay for the drinks. "In case I don't get a chance later to tell you, good luck with it on your honeymoon."

Another Description

One month later, Tom and Steve greeted each other at the same drinking establishment. Colder weather ruled now, but the streets were dry. The holiday season approached, and multicolored lights decorated the window by Tom and Steve's table. They talked about Steve's honeymoon in the Virgin Islands.

After a couple of minutes, Tom asked, "Well, did you try the technique?"

"Yeah," Steve admitted. "It didn't work for me."

"Well, I'm not all that surprised. I probably made a mistake telling you right before your honeymoon, anyway. You probably needed more time to work on it. I hope it didn't spoil your honeymoon."

"No. I remembered what you said. I decided to relax and have fun regardless of whether it worked or not. I tried it twice. I told Laura that I'd read about something I was going to try. After it didn't work for the first couple times, I decided to forget about it and talk to you later. So here I am. I don't think I did anything different than what you told me. I'm not too sure about which muscles we're talking about."

"The technique doesn't work for everybody. I've talked with enough guys to know that. Some guys just have different nerve connections. That doesn't mean there's anything wrong with them. Things feel different for them than for me. When I've needed to explain it to somebody it doesn't work for at first, this is what I tell them. Imagine you're standing at the urinal when someone yells, 'Fire!' Five seconds later they yell, 'Just kidding!' You've stopped urinating, but now you'd like to finish what you started. The muscle you press down on is the same one involved in the technique. At first, you're not using your sphincter for the technique, and that sometimes gets confused in there with the muscles we're talking about. You are using lower abdominal muscles to push down. It could be that you're releasing pressure on the prostate and slowing down your sexual reactions."

"You say this is like pushing down...."

Tom interrupted. "That's the word I use. It feels like down. Remember to push the muscle gradually but so hard for a few seconds that it *automatically* relaxes. The muscle relaxes, not your sphincter. There is, however, a slighter action. That's a contracting in your anal sphincter. In reality, this push consciously against the muscle and the tightening of your anus will occur simultaneously, and about three seconds later the front muscle will automatically relax. Concentrate on the front muscle, though, and worry less about your sphincter muscle."

"So it's like one and two. One—you push down on this muscle until it relaxes automatically?"

"Right."

"And two—you'll feel a contraction in the anus."

"Exactly. It's like a two-step procedure. One and two."

"Like push down in front and contract in back."

"Right, but it's not a big violent thing. Concentrate on precisely the area needed. Don't involve your stomach and holding your breath and straining like you're trying to move your bowels. Some guys have told me they were trying real hard and I told them they probably weren't in touch with the right muscle just because they were distracting themselves with too many other body sensations grunting and straining. It's almost a delicate maneuver. And relaxed, too. Push until relaxation—one. And a slighter contraction in the anus—two. One-two. Nice and easy."

"But I have to repeat this."

"Precisely. You won't want to repeat over and over something difficult and distracting. One-two. Again and again."

"Like in sets?" Steve asked.

"Right. About a fifth of the way through your normal endurance. Do a set of this flexing, one-two, maybe four or five times. I might have told you two or three repetitions. Some guys need more. But do one set of flexing and then about five minutes later repeat it again two or three times. After that, you may need to do it intermittently with longer intervals between using the technique. Eventually, you can sort of tell if you're getting more stimulated and need to slow yourself down. This is what any man who can last a long time does naturally without really thinking about it. We're just doing it consciously now. You have to be in tune with your own reactions and adjust accordingly."

"That helps. I think I was trying too hard and stopping myself."

"That happens," Tom said. "Done correctly, a woman need not know when the man is implementing this at all. It's just a slight muscular thing. One-two."

"Why the two steps?"

"I think it's opening and then closing," Tom explained. "One—you engage a mechanism for slowing the sexual reaction down, delaying an orgasm. Then you have to seal it shut, like locking the blood into the erection. Remember I said you might have a slightly smaller erection. That means you've succeeded. You've locked it in. One is to delay. Two is to seal it in."

"And I should be locked in with an erection that'll

last beyond the time I'm engaged in sex?"

"Yes, if you've done the repetitions enough times. If not, then at some point you'll slip back into your regular pattern of sexual reactions and probably have an orgasm. And that is perfectly all right. You probably prolonged your endurance anyway, and that's what you intended. And don't forget you'll enjoy those building climaxes while you're using the technique although you aren't heading toward an orgasm."

"This may seem like a silly question, but what if I'm successful with this and want to use it most of the time? Won't that affect my ability to have a quickie once in a while?"

"I won't lie to you. It could. I've experienced a few times some difficulty in having an orgasm because I've been using the technique to the exclusion of the old way. Jeannie and I got into a pattern of saving ourselves up for long weekends, and I was too busy during the week to be interested very much. And I did develop a slowness in my reaction. The technique might become a habit, and this habit might require some time for the body to forget. It could be necessary to consciously reprogram your reactions *again* to shorten your timing once the technique becomes a habit. There's two ways to accomplish that. One is just to stop using the technique and let your body regain its inherent memory of the sexual reactions you had before you learned the technique. Also, there is an opposite of the technique."

"I was wondering about that," Steve said. "There are times when you'd like to finish sex sooner and hurry it up."

"And there's something most guys do when they do that. Unfortunately, that's the thing they almost *always* do, and the technique is exactly the opposite. They've trained their bodies to hurry rather than relax and slow down."

"What do they do?"

"They pull on that muscle at first instead of pushing on it. That stimulates the sexual nerve and speeds up the approach of the orgasm."

"That's what I was thinking. I was having trouble because I'm always pulling up instead of pushing."

"You're always in a hurry, right?" Tom asked.

Steve nodded and unconsciously twirled the new wedding band on his left hand. "But you said you can control your timing then?"

"Because I can slow down rather than just always trying to speed up. Eventually you should be able to reacquaint yourself with your body's reactions so you can slow yourself down and maintain an edge on your sexual sensitivity so you'll approach an orgasm when you want to. If you continually repeat the technique, naturally you won't be having an orgasm until you stop at some point."

"Well, that about cleared up what I was wondering about. Laura didn't mind my failure, though. We had a lot of fun without your technique."

"It's not indispensible. Just useful. Good luck with it in your married life anyway."

"I think it will be useful," Steve said.

"Especially if it can help you slow down now and then. Everything we do anymore is in a hurry. If I could persuade people to slow down and enjoy themselves with this technique it would be a major contribution. Probably more important than the technique itself," Tom added.

Sharing Roles

Tom and Steve met several months later at Steve's request. Spring's promise remained unfulfilled, and March dampness invaded the bar whenever someone entered.

As Tom arrived and sat down at the table already occupied by Steve, he remarked, "We always meet in public places to talk about private parts."

"Well, we've both got innocent wives to protect," Steve said.

"Oh?" Tom appeared skeptical.

The waitress took Tom's order and left.

Tom asked, "So what's the addendum to my lecture series that you're proposing?"

"I thought it was going to be a book," Steve said.

"A book later. Right now it's a lecture series."

"Well," Steve explained, "you were saying that after implementing the technique, I'd be locked in until I stopped any form of stimulation. But you also said I could reacquaint myself with my own reactions so I can maintain an edge on my sensitivity. That way I really could control my timing rather than being 'locked in' for a specific length of time. Which is it?"

"It's both. You're beginning to see how the advanced stage—or graduate school, as we called it—works. You don't have to be totally locked in. But I wanted you to learn the basic technique first before you took up the question of timing control."

"But that's what I was starting to think. I could tell that there wasn't just being locked in and not being locked in. There was an intermediate stage of actually controlling or delaying my orgasm to the exact minute I wanted. The key is how many times you push the implementing muscle. That's the key to consciously controlling my timing."

"That's right," Tom said. "It's nice to see my students progressing."

"But it's still a conscious effort. That's not real easy. But I think I'm getting it."

"That's the whole point. Integrating it into the subconscious is the entire goal of my little program. But I can't start people out with that first. It's impossible. First I have to present a conscious exercise for them. That's why I want my pupil first to learn the total endurance time possible. A demonstration of this sort overcomes the skepticism. Next the student has to see how the technique will be a regular part of a formerly uncontrolled reaction. Now we've got a new habit to replace the old pattern. Now you're breaking even that habit to see how you really can consciously control your timing altogether. We've reached the more practical level now."

"This *is* the more practical application," Steve agreed. "First I was at the mercy of my reaction. Then I was totally in control, but it wouldn't go down except by disengaging myself and reading a book or something. Now I think I'm getting to a stage of neither fear of failure, nor nonstop erection but an actual peaceful co-existence with my own reactions. I can darn well control how long I want to last."

"It just depends on how many times you flex that muscle. Since that's an individual reaction, I don't tell guys a magic number because I'd probably be wrong."

"It's different now with Laura," Steve said. "We've

started to decide the time we want to spend making love, still knowing we'll end up satisfied at the end anyway."

"Good. You've probably noticed you have a different role now, huh?"

"I do," Steve agreed. "You mentioned something before about traditional roles being switched, that women could always outlast men. I've been real good not abusing this ability. And we are talking about it as well as doing it. I'm not dominant anymore because I have to decide how long to last, and Laura has to help me make that decision. She tells me while we're making love. We never did that before."

Tom nodded. "Women's two strengths in the past have been sexual dominance and nurturing. If everyone starts using the technique, those two virtues will have to be shared between the sexes equally."

"Maybe women won't dominate the bed anymore," Steve said.

"They won't, but then men won't dominate the business world, either. Males may not have to fight an ego problem with their own sexual self-image, and their frustrations and aggressions won't have to carry over into their jobs. They won't have to prove themselves anymore, because they will have proved their ability to themselves.

"This ego problem is quite a burden to carry. And they'll find out what a problem it is when they've relieved themselves of it. They won't have to establish their worth in society. They'll be able to accept their sexuality. Sex won't be an issue anymore. Their relationship will be more important than their sex drive.

"Having accepted themselves, men may discover a whole new dimension to life they've never looked at before. In the past, they may have bottled up some insecurity and hurt others."

Tom stopped and smiled as a thought came to him.

"We'll all benefit from those changes," he continued. "In bed, women used to protect our egos. 'We'll just snuggle. That's okay,' they'd tell a man who was impotent at some time. Now men may need to do that if a woman doesn't want prolonged lovemaking. Men will have to learn an understanding of women and their giving nature. Men will have to open themselves mentally to the approach women have always taken."

Steve commented, "That reminds me of two neat ladies I know. One's a dental assistant and the other sells real estate. Both are not your hard-driving career climbers. They really do want to *help* people first. The dental hygienist wants her patient to be comfortable, and the lady in real estate really doesn't talk someone into a deal that isn't right for them. They don't operate in the traditional manner, but people seem to realize that these ladies do a better job than any man could."

"And that's precisely why. The quality of their work becomes the goal rather than their own personal gain. Accommodating another person's needs rather than your own is the mark of a better human being. And historically most of the jerks have been men. And most saints exhibit feminine qualities," Tom added.

"Well," Steve said, "that's what I've learned about being married. I'm not getting many opportunities to be a jerk anymore."

Tom laughed. "That's a real secret no one should let out. Who'd get married then? People resist their own growth. But that's probably the basic reason for getting married. You get tired of your old self, don't you?"

"I don't remember the old me too well."

"That's the whole point," Tom said. "The technique will help people evolve and get closer together, the same function marriage fulfills. A hundred years from now, no one may remember what it was like before the technique came along."